I0643886

KNOWLEDGE ENCYCLOPEDIA

# OCEAN & WATERBODIES

# OUR PLANET EARTH



Wonder House

(An imprint of Prakash Books)

contact@wonderhousebooks.com

**Disclaimer:** The information contained in this encyclopedia has been collated with inputs from subject experts. All information contained herein is true to the best of the Publisher's knowledge. Maps are only indicative in nature.

ISBN : 9789354402166

# Table of Contents

# THE GREAT **OCEAN**

**Earth is the only planet in the solar system to have stable bodies of liquid water on the surface.** 70 per cent of its surface is covered with water. This vast, salty, and continuous body of water is called the ocean. Apart from the ocean, there are other waterbodies on Earth. They come in different shapes and sizes from seas to rivers, lakes, ponds, bays, gulfs, and straits. These are much smaller than the oceans and each of them contain a different ecosystem with plants, animals, and fish unique to their environment.

Most of the above-mentioned waterbodies are naturally formed geographical features with some exceptions. There are some small waterbodies that are artificial and contained. These along with some smaller waterbodies that are not contained are navigable and referred to as waterways.

▼ *The ocean is a great resource for human beings as it provides water, food, and a source of transportation.*

# What is an Ocean?

**Oceans make a continuous body of salt water covering 70 per cent of Earth's surface.** Oceans contain almost 98 per cent of all water on Earth. Ocean water is salty due to the presence of a chemical substance called **sodium chloride** or salt. More than 95 per cent of our oceans are still unexplored.

▲ *There is so much salt in the ocean that if you took it all out and spread it evenly over the planet's surface, it would form a layer more than 152 metres in height*

▼ *There is enough water in the oceans to fill up a cube whose edges are 1,000 kilometres in length*

## Formation

This vast body of water makes Earth different from other planets in the solar system. Oceans have been present on Earth's surface for about four billion years, carving the coastline, driving the climate, and controlling life. However, 4.5 billion years ago, when Earth was born, it was a molten **inferno**. There was no place for liquid water, but the elements to create water were present deep within the newly formed planet. When the first volcanoes erupted, the gas that came out was steam. Later, molten rocks cooled and clouds formed. Consequently, it rained for centuries and filled the basins that are now our oceans.

## In Real Life

Half of the oxygen present in the atmosphere is produced from ocean water.

## Threat to Oceans

Despite the fact that oceans provide useful materials, they are prone to damage due to overfishing, pollution, etc. **Overfishing** means that people take too many fish from the water, too quickly; even faster than they can naturally be replaced. It is important to take care of aquatic ecosystems because their loss spells consequences for all living beings. The climate and weather, the air we breathe, the food we eat, all depend on oceans. Oceans are the most important source of nourishment for all the different kinds of life on Earth.

▲ *The ocean, which is home to many species of fish, has been polluted by human activities over the years*

## Names of Oceans

There are five major oceans. These are the Pacific Ocean, the Indian Ocean, the Atlantic Ocean, the Arctic Ocean, and the Antarctic or Southern Ocean. The fifth ocean is the newest one considered by the International Hydrographic Organisation (IHO). However, the three major oceans of the world are the Pacific, the Atlantic, and the Indian Oceans. They are called the three great oceans. Different cultures had different names for them through the ages, but the current names were first made a long time ago—as early as 450 BCE for the Atlantic, and in the 1500s for the others.

*The map marks all the continents and the surrounding oceans. Actually, Earth has only one continuous ocean but it is demarcated according to landmasses*

### Isn't It Amazing!

Water in the ocean is constantly and continuously moving. It is like a conveyor belt in a factory. So, the global ocean conveyor belt is the name given to the system of constantly moving and circulating water. This movement is driven by salinity and temperature.

*Over the years, ports have come to be hubs of human activities*

## Releasing Water

Rainfall made up only half of our present oceans. According to some scientists, the rest of the water came from space. During Earth's formative years, it was hit by thousands of **comets** which were made of ice. When the downpour stopped, Earth filled up with thousands of litres of water.

Water has always been present in Earth's mantle. It was gradually released after volcanic eruptions. In fact, water is still being released from Earth's mantle after volcanic eruptions.

The water in the oceans is attracted to the surface due to the gravitational pull of Earth. It cannot leave the planet through natural means.

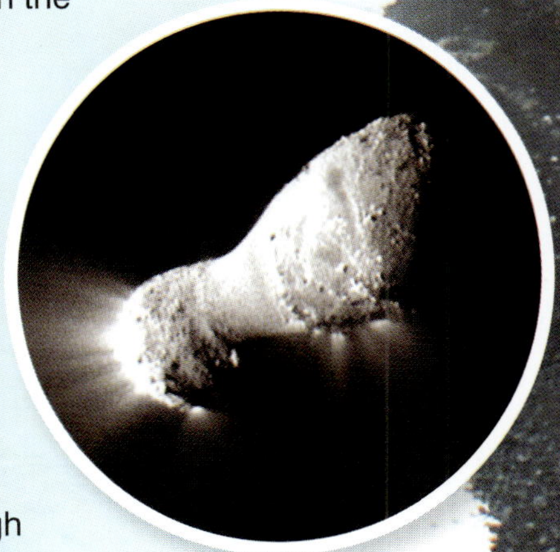

*A comet is filled with dust, rock, and ice. They are informally called "dirty snowballs"*

# Peeling Back Layers

**Scientists have divided the ocean into five main layers.** These layers are known as zones. They extend from the surface to the most extreme depths where light cannot penetrate.

The ocean deep zones are where some of the most fascinating creatures are found. As the depth of an ocean increases, the temperature drops at an extraordinary rate. However, the pressure increases. Each of the ocean's layers have their own characteristics.

*Kelp is a seaweed found underwater near coastal regions*

## Epipelagic Zone

The epipelagic zone, also known as the sunlight zone of the ocean, starts from the water's surface and extends for 200 metres. There is plenty of light and heat within this layer and most oceanic life and human activities occur here. However, both light and heat decrease as the depth increases. The pressure here is low, but it increases with depth. Coral reefs can be found in this layer. Photosynthesis for aquatic plants can only happen in this level.

## Bathypelagic Zone

The next layer is called the bathypelagic zone, also known as the midnight zone. This zone is dark, with the only visible light coming from its aquatic animals. Some examples of the animals found here are the pelican eel and humpback anglerfish. The penetration of sunlight is very low, hence many animals in this layer are either black or red. This is for their defence because only minute amounts of blue-green light reach this zone. The colour red and black are not reflected in this light. Some whale species, such as the sperm whale, spend some time at this level in search of food.

*The sperm whale occasionally hunts in the bathypelagic zone*

## In Real Life

The lowest and the deepest point on Earth is the Mariana Trench. It is found in the floor of the western North Pacific Ocean. The Mariana Trench stretches for more than 2,550 kilometres with a mean width of 69 kilometres. The greatest depths are reached in the Challenger Deep at 11,034 metres. The Mariana Trench was designated as US national monument in 2009 as it is within the territories of US dependencies.

## Isn't It Amazing!

Earth's longest chain of mountains, the Mid-Ocean Ridge, is almost entirely beneath the ocean. It is a continuous range of underwater volcanoes that wraps around the globe like seam on a baseball. It stretches nearly 65,000 kilometres. The majority of the system is underwater, with an average water depth to the top of the ridge of 2,500 metres.

## Mesopelagic Zone

Below the epipelagic zone lies the mesopelagic zone or the twilight zone. It starts 200 metres from the surface and extends to 1,000 metres from the surface. This twilight or mid-water zone is home to some aquatic animals like the swordfish and wolf eel. Sunlight here is sparse, but the light of bioluminescent creatures is visible. A diverse set of fish including swordfish, squid, and cuttlefish, can be found here.

## Abyssopelagic Zone

The abyssopelagic zone is also known as the abyss. The name originates from the Greek word '*abyssus*' meaning 'bottomless'. In this zone, the temperatures are near freezing point and there is no penetration of natural light. As there is no sunlight, there are no plants. Three-fifths of the ocean floor falls within this zone.

*Animals like the abyssal octopus and tripod fish, etc., are found in the abyssopelagic zone*

## Hadalpelagic Zone

The ocean trenches are found in the hadalpelagic zone. This zone begins 6,000 metres from the surface and extends to the deepest parts of the ocean floor. The depth of this layer depends on the trenches and valleys in the area. In Puerto Rico, fish were discovered as deep as 8,369 metres. The pressure exerted at this zone is equal to that of 48 jet planes.

*The grenadier fish are the most abundant fish found in this zone*

# The Five Major Oceans

**There is only one true ocean on Earth.** This connected body of water surrounds the seven continents. It has been demarcated into five oceans by scientists so that they can study and understand them better. These are the Pacific, Atlantic, Indian, Arctic, and the Southern Ocean.

## Why are Oceans Blue?

The water in the ocean appears blue because sunlight falls on it. Sunlight is white light. The water absorbs the red, orange, and yellow wavelengths from this white light more strongly than it does the blue wavelengths. In fact, it even reflects these blue wavelengths. That is why the ocean water and sky appear blue.

*The map marks the five major oceans of the world*

## Incredible Individuals

Film director James Cameron has made a number of trips and expeditions to the ocean deep. He has dived on the wreck of the Titanic multiple times, and is 1 of 4 people who have made their way to the depth of the Challenger Deep, the deepest point in the Mariana Trench.

## The Pacific Ocean

The Pacific Ocean is the biggest ocean in the world. It covers more than 30 per cent of Earth's surface. The name 'Pacific' comes from the Latin word '*pacificus*', meaning 'peaceful ocean'. However, it is not that calm and peaceful, as the Ring of Fire is located near it. There are too many volcanoes in this region, and volcanic eruptions occur quite frequently along with earthquakes.

*75 per cent of the world's active volcanoes are located in the Pacific Ocean basin*

*The photograph shows a part of the Atlantic Ocean Road, an 8.3 kilometres road that connects the island of Averøy, Norway, with the mainland*

## The Atlantic Ocean

The Atlantic is the second-biggest ocean in the world and lies between the continents of America, Europe, and Africa. It is about half the size of the Pacific Ocean, covering roughly 20 per cent of Earth's surface. It was mentioned for the first time in 450 BCE as '*Atlantis thalassa*' in the book *The Histories* by Herodotus, meaning the 'Sea of Atlas'.

## The Arctic Ocean

The Arctic ocean is the smallest and shallowest among the major oceans. It is located entirely within the Arctic Circle and covers around 4 per cent of Earth's surface. It occupies the region of the North Pole. Once called the Frozen Ocean, most of the Arctic Ocean is covered with ice throughout the year.

*The Arctic Ocean's name is derived from the Greek word 'arktikos', which means 'bear'*

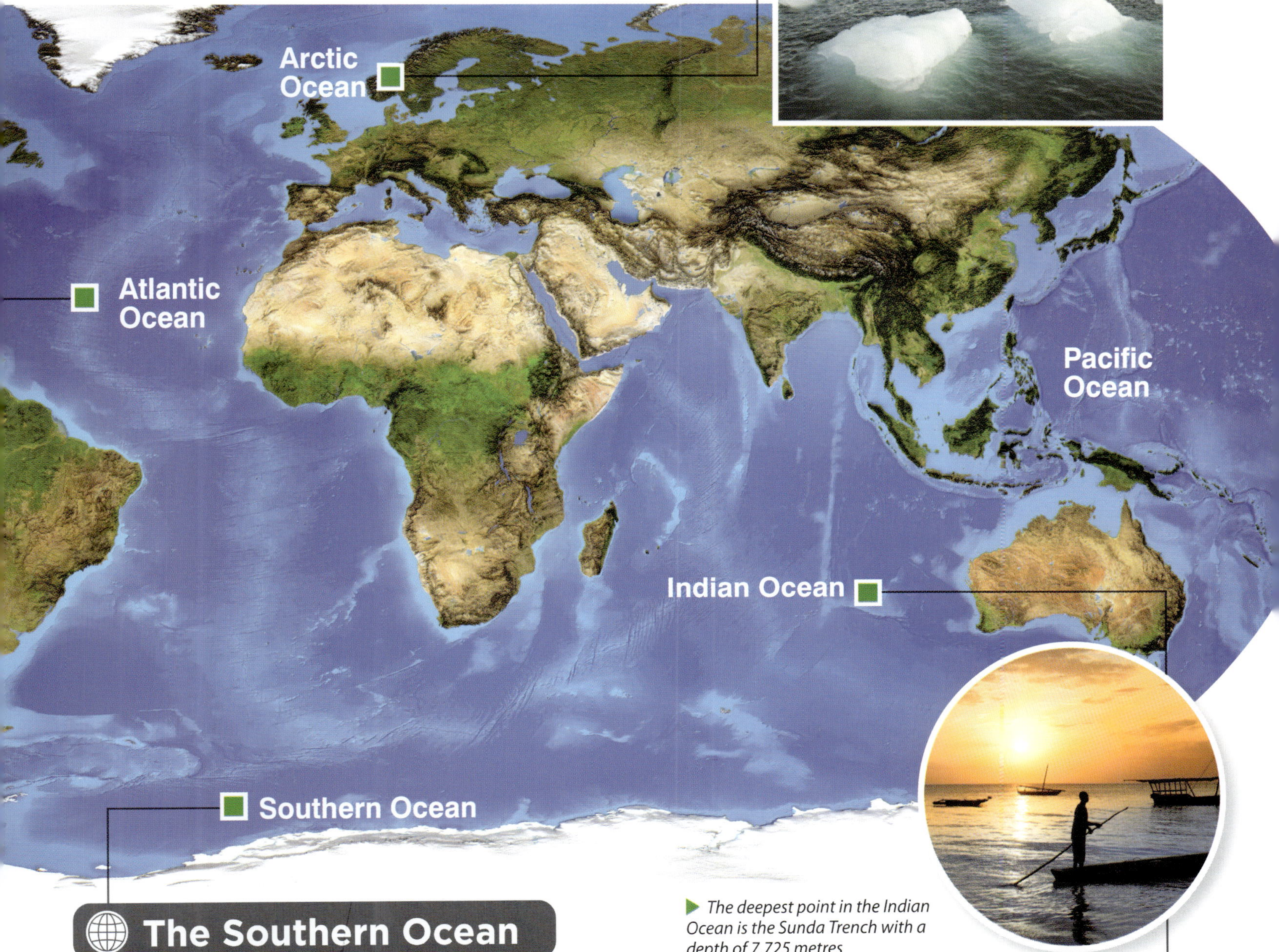


## The Southern Ocean

The Antarctic Ocean was recently renamed as the Southern Ocean. The Atlantic, Indian, and Pacific Ocean basins merge into icy waters around Antarctica. It is the fourth-largest ocean located at the southernmost point of the planet and surrounds Antarctica. The Southern Ocean is the least explored and least understood marine region in the world.

*The Southern Ocean has the largest ocean current flowing from the west to the east, and is called the Antarctic Circumpolar Current*

*The deepest point in the Indian Ocean is the Sunda Trench with a depth of 7,725 metres*

## The Indian Ocean

The Indian Ocean covers one-fifth of the world's oceans and is the third largest after the Pacific and the Atlantic Oceans. It is geologically the youngest and physically the most complex among the three major oceans. The Indian Ocean is bounded by Australia in the East, by Africa in the West, by Asia in the North and the Atlantic Ocean in the South. It is said to be the warmest ocean of all.

# Life in the Ocean

**The term 'marine life' refers to all the living organisms living in Earth's waters.** These include a diverse array of plants, animals, and other organisms such as **bacteria** and **archaea**. It is believed that about one million species of animals live in the ocean. Among these, 95 per cent are invertebrates such as jellyfish and shrimp.

## Incredible Individuals

Marie Lebour (1876–1971) was a British marine biologist (a person who studies marine life in great detail). She researched the life cycles of different marine animals like molluscs and microplankton. She discovered 28 new species of microplankton which she described in her written works. She also conducted research on the eggs and larval stages of herrings and sprats.

## Flora

An ocean is a large and deep body of water. Plants and animals are found in all different parts of the oceans except for regions where there is no sunlight. Marine plants provide food, shelter, and protection for the animals. One can find great diversity in the flora of the ocean, from **microscopic** plankton to the *Nymphaeaceae*, a giant species of the water lily plant.

There are two types of plants found in the ocean—rooted plants and floating plants. Rooted plants, as the name suggests, are plants whose roots are attached to the ocean floor. They need sunlight, so they grow near the shores and in shallow waters. Floating plants drift freely without attached roots. They grow on the water's surface.

*Seaweeds are used in foods, fertilisers and cosmetics. They also have medicinal value*

A majority of the plants are tiny algae called phytoplankton. All these microscopic plants have a big job to do. They produce half the world's oxygen, which human beings and all other organisms require for survival. There are some bigger algae in the water called seaweed and kelp. We can even find forests in the ocean called kelp forests. They are present in cold and shallow waters. These big plants provide food and shelter to a variety of marine life.

*Sea lily*

ome species of
fish are immortal. For
nple, the immortal
fish—Turritopsis
rnii—found in the
literranean Sea and
e waters of Japan
not die of old age

▶ Nekton, such as dolphins, can live in both shallow and deep ocean waters

## Fauna

Fish, sponges, sea anemones, and corals are some examples of marine animals. Crustaceans are invertebrates that have exoskeletons. They are also considered to be marine animals. Crabs, shrimp, and lobsters are examples of crustaceans. But marine diversity is not just limited to fish and crustaceans, even some mammals live in the water. Dolphins, porpoises, and manatees are examples of marine mammals. A common vertebrate found in the ocean is the bristlemouth fish. It is a tiny ocean fish that glows in the dark and has needle-like fangs.

▲ Shrimp caught from the ocean

Marine animals can be divided into three groups—zooplankton, nektons, and benthos. The word plankton originates from the Greek word '*planktos*', which means 'wandering'. Zooplankton, such as jellyfish, are drifting or floating animals. They are very small. It is difficult to see these creatures with the naked eye. Nektons are free swimmers and most of the ocean animals belong to this class. Octopuses, dolphins, whales, eels, squids, and sharks are examples of nektons. Benthos are the animals that spend their entire lives at the bottom of the ocean. Lobsters, oysters, and some species of worms and snails are examples of benthos.

▼ Coral reefs show some of the greatest bio-diversity in the world, enough so that we are still finding new species

### Isn't It Amazing!

The eel uses its shock to stun its prey, and keep predators at bay. The shock of an electric eel has been known to knock a horse off its feet. Now that's shocking!

▲ Electric eel

# The Ocean in Motion

**The water in the ocean is never still.** It is constantly moving from north to south, east to west, and up and down the shores around the world. These movements can be influenced by the movement and force of local winds. The ocean's movements can also be influenced by the Earth's rotation and revolution, as well as the position of the Moon and the Sun in relation to the Earth. These different movements are categorised as waves, tides, and ocean currents. The movements are also influenced by the temperature, salinity, and **density** of water.

▲ *The waves hit a road built over the ocean*

## Waves

Waves create oscillatory movements that cause the rise and fall of surface water. These are horizontal movements. Waves are created by energy, which moves across the ocean's surface. This energy is provided by the winds. The winds transfer energy to the water on the ocean's surface.

The transfer of that energy may create tiny ripples that disappear when the winds die down. Or, the energy may create larger waves that continue until they reach the shore. Each water particle moves in a circular manner in waves. There are two parts of a wave, the raised part is called the crest and the lower part is called the trough. Waves are measured by their wavelengths, that is the horizontal distance between the crests.

## Ocean Currents

An ocean current is a continuous, directed movement of ocean water generated by a number of forces acting upon the water, such as the wind, the Earth's rotation, temperature, and salinity. The ocean currents that are driven by winds move clockwise in the Northern Hemisphere and counter-clockwise in the Southern Hemisphere. As the water moves in these ocean currents, it brings cold water towards the Equator on the west coasts. At the same time, it brings warm water towards the poles on the east coasts. Ocean currents occur in all the major oceans. The Gulf Stream in the Atlantic Ocean is an ocean current.

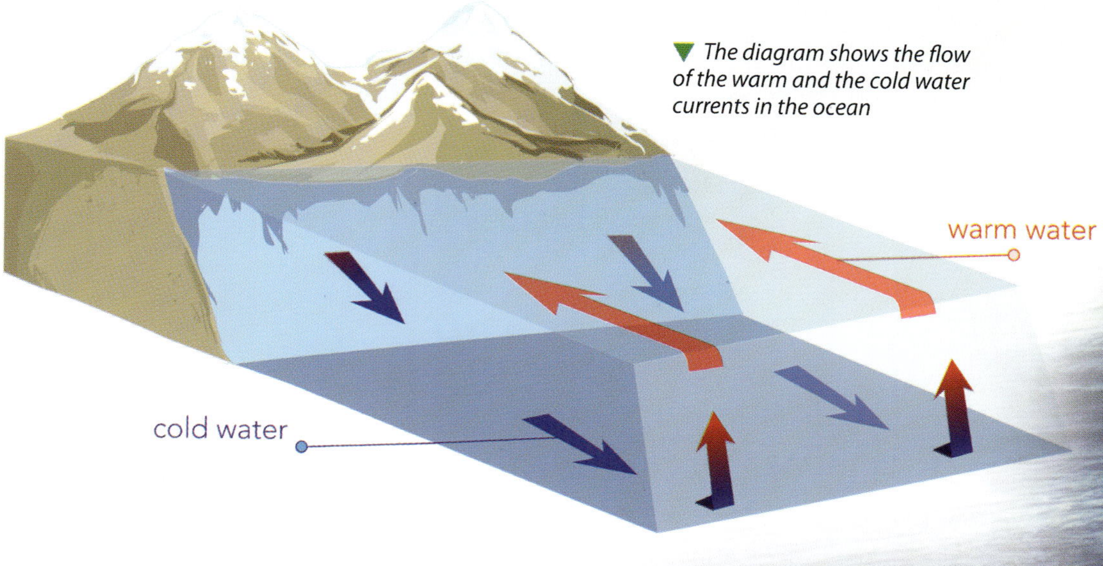


▼ *The diagram shows the flow of the warm and the cold water currents in the ocean*

## Types of Ocean Currents

There are two types of ocean currents—warm ocean currents and cold ocean currents. Ocean currents that flow from the equatorial regions towards the poles and have a higher surface temperature are called warm ocean currents. They move warm waters to the cool regions. In the Northern Hemisphere, they are found on the west coasts of the continents in the higher latitudes, for example, the Alaskan and Norwegian Currents.

Ocean currents that flow from the polar regions towards the Equator and have a lower surface temperature are called cold currents. They carry cold water towards the warmer regions. They occur on the west coasts of the continents in the low and middle latitudes of both hemispheres. In the Northern Hemisphere, they are found on the east coast in the higher latitudes, for example, the Labrador, East Greenland, and Oyashio Currents.

### Isn't It Amazing!

Earth tides are deformations of the solid earth caused by the sun and moon's periodic gravitational attractions. They occur on a regular basis due to the Earth's rotation in the solar and lunar gravitational fields. The lunar-solar attractions often cause elastic deformations in the solid earth, causing the Earth's shape to change and the vertical to be distorted.

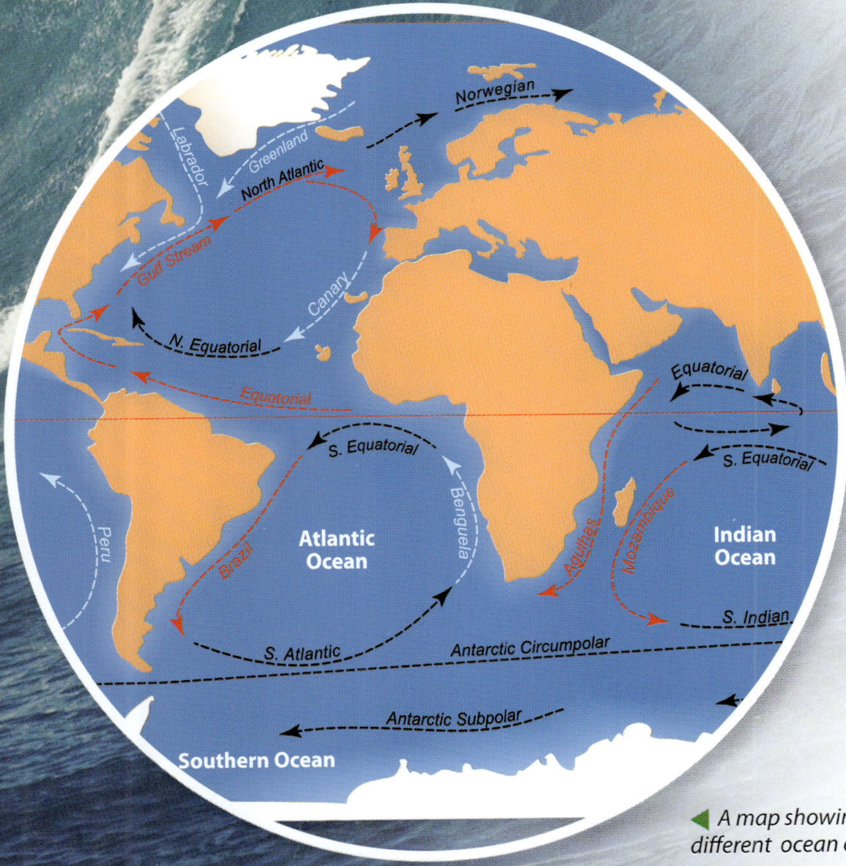


*A map showing different ocean currents*

## Tides

*High tide meter*

The movement of a tide is the periodic rise and fall of water, which occurs once or twice in a day. These are vertical movements of water caused mainly due to the gravitational pull of Earth's Moon. The greatest height reached as the water rises is known as high tide or flood tide. The lowest level reached as the water falls is known as low tide or ebb. Tides are classified according to their frequency or the position of the Sun, Earth and Moon when they occur.

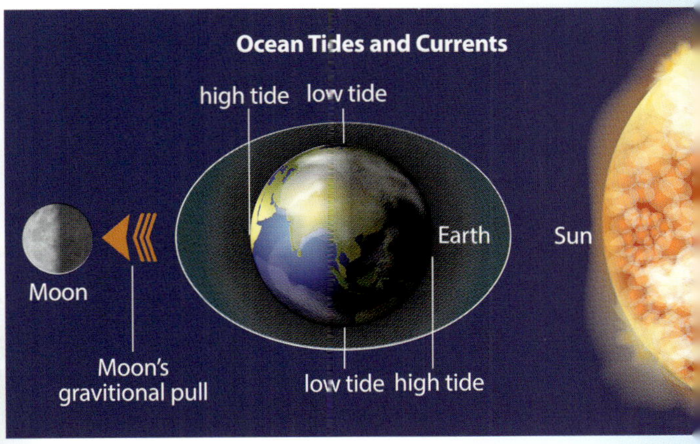


*The diagram shows how the position of the moon and its gravitational pull influence high tide and low tide on Earth*

## Types of Tides

Tides based on frequency are the semi-diurnal tide, diurnal tide, and mixed tide. Semi-diurnal tides are the most common, featuring two high tides and two low tides each day. The diurnal tides feature only one high tide and one low tide each day. The mixed tides have variations in heights. These are common along the western coast of North America.

When the Sun, Moon, and Earth are in a straight line, the height of the tide is higher than normal. This is known as a spring tide. On the other hand, after seven days of the spring tide, when the Moon and the Sun stand at right angles with regard to Earth's position, the tides are lower than normal.
This is known as the neap tide.

# Importance of Oceans

**Oceans cover roughly three-fourths of our planet.** They are of great importance not only to human beings but to each and every living organism on Earth. Surprisingly, oceans are the world's largest producer of food. They also provide minerals, oil, and natural gas. They produce more than half the world's oxygen and absorb carbon dioxide. It is estimated that oceans produce around 50–80 per cent of the oxygen on Earth and absorb almost one third of the carbon dioxide emitted. Oceans and ocean currents maintain the global climate by absorbing heat from the Sun.

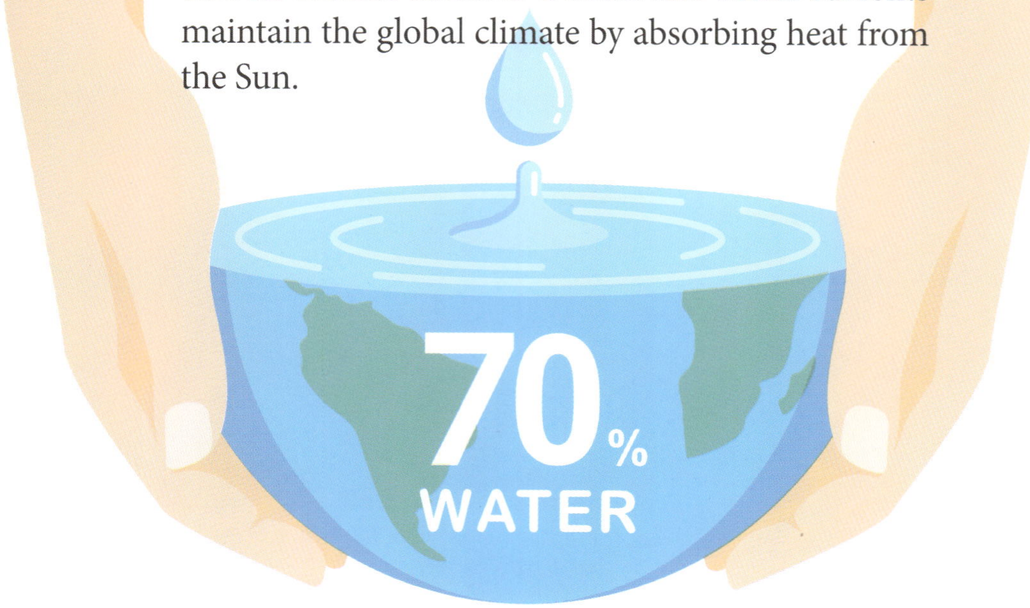


## Regulating Climate

Oceans regulate the climate on Earth in many ways. The water soaks up heat and transports the warm water from the Equator to the poles, and cold water from the poles to the tropics by the movement of the ocean currents. Without these movements, the global climate would have been inhospitable.

▲ *The fishing industry worldwide employs around 200 million people*

## Food Source

Oceans are a great source of protein as they contain many different species of fish that are consumed by billions of people. Algae and sea plants are used for cooking delicacies such as sushi. It is believed that there are more than 2.2 million different species of animals that live underwater. It is possible that there are species of animals yet to be discovered.

## Occupation

Statistics reveal that 59.6 million people around the world are engaged in fishing and **aquaculture**. Therefore, oceans are a source of income for many. However, our oceans are facing major threats due to global warming, pollution, habitat destruction, invasive species, and a dramatic decrease in ocean fish stocks. These threats to the oceans are so extensive that more than 40 per cent of the ocean area has been severely affected and no area has been left untouched. It is therefore important for us to protect oceans.

### In Real Life

There is a component in phytoplankton known as beta-carotene. It can protect the corneas of our eyes and has a lot of minerals that can improve our vision.

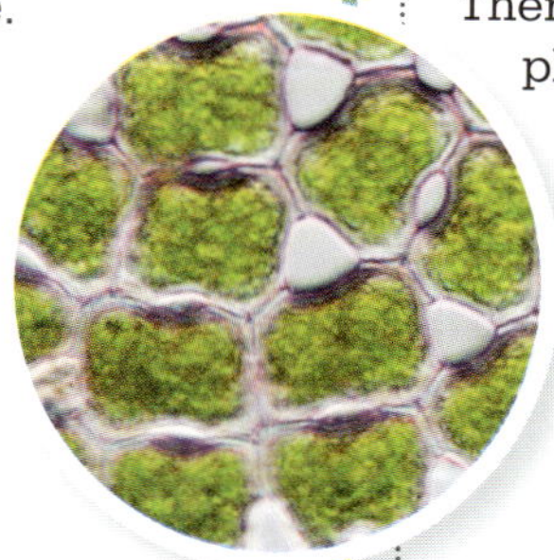

◀ *Phytoplankton is incredibly nutritious*

## Oxygen

Though there are no trees in the oceans, algae and phytoplankton act as trees and fill the atmosphere with ample oxygen. These organisms may be microscopic, but they do a very important task.

# Sources of Water

**There are many types of waterbodies on Earth.** They may be saltwater or fresh water. Some of these may be moving and some are contained. They can be distinguished by their shapes, sizes, and vegetation. Sources of water can be broadly divided into two categories: surface water and groundwater. Surface water is found in oceans, seas, lakes, rivers, ponds, and reservoirs. Groundwater lies under land surface that travels through and fills openings in the rocks. The rocks that store and transmit groundwater are called aquifers.

*Seawater is salty, like ocean water*

## Surface Water

It is a body of water that is above the ground, such as oceans, streams, rivers, lakes, wetlands, reservoirs, and creeks. Surface water moves to and from the Earth's surface through the water cycle. Precipitation and water runoff feed bodies of surface water.

There are three types of surface water: perennial, ephemeral, and man-made. Perennial type of source is permanent that persists throughout the year and is refilled with groundwater when there is little precipitation. Rivers, lakes, streams, and ponds are some examples of perennial surface water.

Ephemeral (semi-permanent) surface water exists for only part of the year. This surface water includes small creeks, lagoons, and water holes. Man-made surface water is found in artificial structures, such as dams and constructed wetlands.

The availability of surface water is naturally more than the groundwater. Therefore, it can be used for drinking, cooking, bathing, and agricultural activities. Wetlands with surface water are also important habitats for aquatic plants and wildlife.

*A view of the Bay of Bengal*

## Groundwater

These sources are found beneath the land surface, such as springs and wells. In the water cycle we can observe that when rain falls to the ground, some water flows along the land to the streams or lakes, other water evaporates into the atmosphere, while some is taken up by plants, and the remaining seeps into the ground. Water that seeps deep into the ground is called groundwater. It is formed as water flows through the earth's surface and passes through rock voids. Groundwater and surface water are also reservoirs that can feed into one another. Groundwater can resurface on land to replenish surface water, while surface water can seep underground to become groundwater. These are the places where springs form.

*Ponds support two-th.rds of all fresh water species*

# The Splendid Seas

**A sea is a large area of salt water that may or may not connect to an ocean.** The Caribbean Sea connects to the Atlantic Ocean. However, the Caspian Sea is landlocked. Many consider the Caspian Sea to be a lake because like other seas it does not drain into the ocean but it is sea-like in its size and depth. Some of the major seas of the world are the Mediterranean Sea, the Black Sea, and the Arabian Sea.

*Previously, the Black Sea was named 'inhospitable sea' by the Greeks as it was difficult to navigate*

## The Black Sea

The Black Sea is oval-shaped and lies in south-eastern Europe. Though it lies deep inland, it is connected with the Atlantic Ocean through a series of waterways. They are the Bosporus Strait and the Sea of Marmara. The Dardanelles Strait links the Black Sea to the Aegean Sea, the Mediterranean Sea, and the Atlantic Ocean. The Black Sea is located at the point where Europe and Asia meet. Its bordering countries are Ukraine, Russia, Georgia, Turkey, Bulgaria, and Romania. Rivers like the Danube, Dniester, Bug, Dnieper, Don, and Kuban empty into the Black Sea.

## The Mediterranean Sea

The Mediterranean is a large, intercontinental sea that separates Europe from Africa. It stretches from the Atlantic Ocean in the west to Asia in the east. This sea is called the sea between lands.

The Mediterranean Sea is deep and almost landlocked. It lies between latitudes 30° and 46° N and longitudes 5°50′ W and 36° E. The Strait of Gibraltar connects the Mediterranean Sea with the Atlantic Ocean. The area of the Mediterranean is 25,12,000 square kilometres. It is of historical importance as many early civilisations developed in the Mediterranean region. Therefore, it is also described as the cradle of civilisation.

*The picture shows a coast of the Mediterranean Sea in Europe. It is active with beachgoers and boating enthusiasts*

## In Real Life

The Caspian Sea receives water from the Volga, Ural, Emba, Kura, and Terek Rivers, among others, but has no outlet. About 130 rivers drain their waters into the Caspian Sea.

*The Caspian Sea lies east of the Caucasus Mountains at Europe's south-easternmost extremity*

## The Caspian Sea

As it is landlocked, the Caspian Sea is the world's largest inland body of water. It lies between Europe and Asia, bordering Russia and Azerbaijan in the west, Kazakhstan in the north, Turkmenistan in the east and Iran in the south. It dominates west-central Asia. The area of the Caspian Sea is approximately 3,86,400 square kilometres, which is larger than Japan. The sea was named for the Kaspi, the ancient people who once lived on its western shores. Among its other historical names, Khazarsk and Khvalynsk were derived from the former people of the region, while Girkansk stems from Girkanos, which means the 'country of wolves'.

## The Arabian Sea

The Arabian Sea is located in the north-western part of the Indian Ocean. It covers an area of 38,62,000 square kilometres and its depth is 8,970 feet. It forms a part of the principal sea route between Europe and India. It is also bounded on the north by Pakistan and Iran, and on the west by the Horn of Africa. In Roman times its name was Erythraean Sea. Some of the islands in the sea are Socotra in Yemen, Lakshadweep in India, and Kuria Muria off the coast of Oman. The Indus and the Narmada are two major rivers that drain into the Arabian Sea.

*Mumbai, India, is one of the busiest ports in the Arabian Sea*

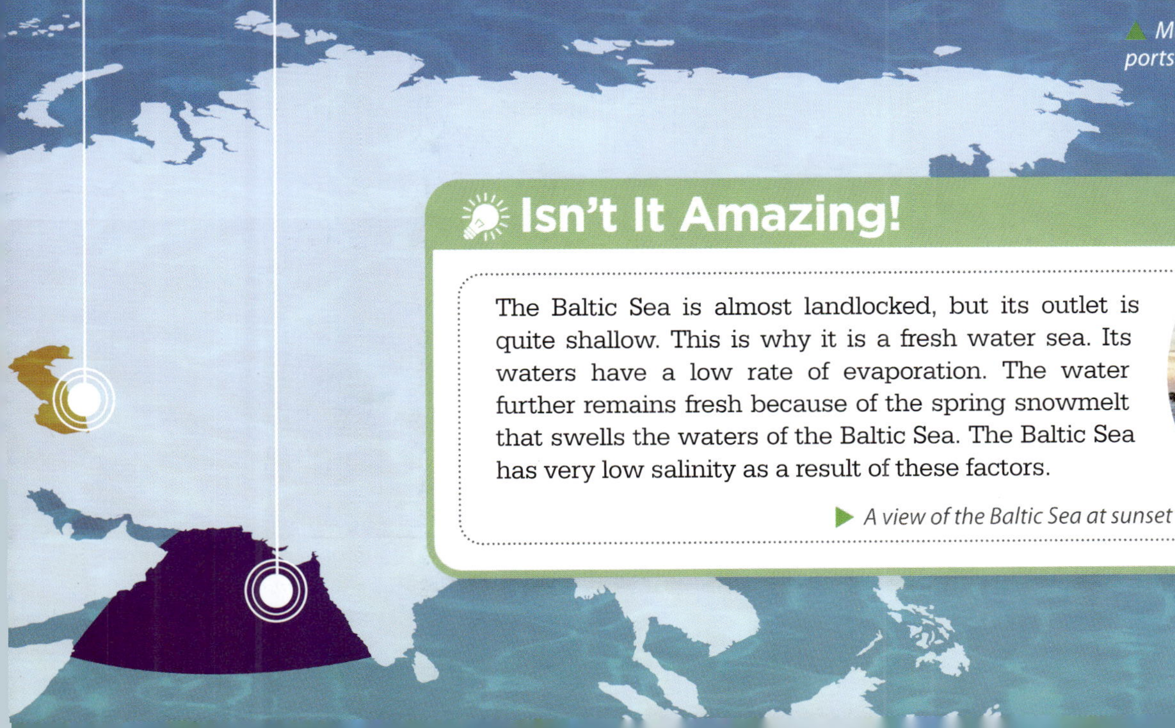

## Isn't It Amazing!

The Baltic Sea is almost landlocked, but its outlet is quite shallow. This is why it is a fresh water sea. Its waters have a low rate of evaporation. The water further remains fresh because of the spring snowmelt that swells the waters of the Baltic Sea. The Baltic Sea has very low salinity as a result of these factors.

*A view of the Baltic Sea at sunset*

# Home to History

**Early civilisations grew along rivers.** Since the pre-historic age, rivers attracted human beings looking to settle in one place. Early settlers realised that lands along rivers were fertile enough to cultivate crops. They grew crops and stored the surplus, eliminating the need to move from place to place in search of food. They formed permanent settlements which grew into famous ancient civilisations like the Mesopotamian, Indus Valley, Nile River Valley, and the Yellow River civilisations. These further became the basis for states, nations, and empires.

*The land around Rivers Tigris and Euphrates is still very fertile. As there was an abundance of water, people of the Mesopotamian Civilisation developed farming and irrigation systems*

*The Nile River flooded every year in August and provided nutrients to the soil for growing crops in the dry desert land of Egypt*

*The Euphrates River rises in eastern Turkey and flows through Syria and Iraq*

## Tigris & Euphrates Rivers

The Tigris-Euphrates river system in southwest Asia constitutes these two rivers. They flow parallel to each other through the Middle East. Their source is in Turkey, 80 kilometres apart. They travel through northern Syria and Iraq towards the Persian Gulf. The length of River Euphrates is 2,800 kilometres. On the other hand, River Tigris is not as long as the Euphrates. It is about 1,850 kilometres long. Many civilisations have grown along the banks of these rivers. The most famous and prominent one was the Mesopotamian Civilisation which stretched from c. 5000–3500 BCE.

## The Nile River

The Nile River is located in southeast Africa and has been recognised as the longest river on Earth. It rises south of the Equator and flows northward through northeast Africa to drain into the Mediterranean Sea. It has a length of about 6,650 kilometres. This mighty river has two main tributaries which meet to form the Nile. One tributary is called the White Nile, which starts in South Sudan. The other is called the Blue Nile, and that starts in Ethiopia.

This river has been very important from the perspective of human history. It provided a fertile soil for cultivation. The river therefore played an essential role in the growth of the ancient Egyptian Civilisation around c. 3100 BCE.

## The Indus River

The Indus River, also known as Sindhu in Sanskrit, is a river in South Asia. It is one of the longest rivers in the world, with a length of 3,200 kilometres. It flows from Tibet, into Jammu and Kashmir, and then into Pakistan. The main tributaries of the Indus River are the Rivers Kabul and Kurram on the right bank; and the Jhelum, Chenab, Ravi, Beas, and the Sutlej Rivers on the left bank. The Indus Valley Civilisation grew around this river around c. 4000–3000 BCE. It had highly developed cities with a famous underground drainage system.

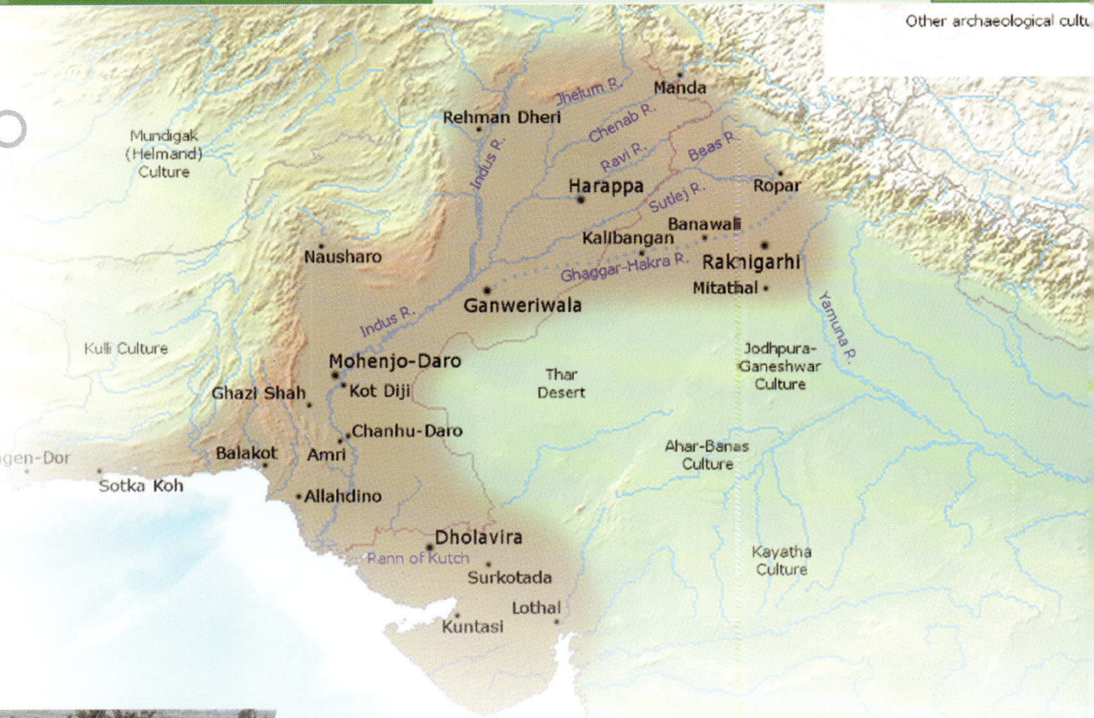


*The map shows the extent of the Indus Valley Civilisation at its peak, with clear markings of River Indus and its tributaries*

*Ruins of two big cities of the Indus Valley Civilisation, Mohenjo-Daro and Harappa*

*The length of the Yellow River is 5,463 kilometres. The area of its drainage basin is around 750,000 square kilometres*

### In Real Life

The Indus River displays a unique phenomenon called **tidal bore**. It is a giant wave which moves forward from the sea onto the rivers along with an unusual tide. It enters shallow and narrow inlets and can cause a lot of destruction.

## The Yellow River

The Hwang Ho River in China, also known as the Yellow River, is the third largest river in Asia. It is the principal river in China and is called the 'cradle of Chinese civilisation'.

The Hwang Ho River rises on the plateau of Tibet and flows eastward, emptying into the Yellow Sea. It stretches across China for more than 4,667 kilometres. It carries yellow-coloured silt all the way hence the name. The river and its tributaries played a vital role in shaping the Chinese civilisation.

# The Grand Rivers

**A river is a large, natural stream of flowing water.** There are many rivers flowing through the continents. However, some rivers flow throughout the year, whereas there are some that are filled only in the wet seasons. Rivers that have uninterrupted flow throughout the year are called perennial rivers, while the rivers that flow in the monsoon season are called seasonal rivers. Rivers Mississippi, Amazon, Indus, Congo, and Ganga are all perennial. Rivers Mahanadi, Godavari, Krishna, and Kaveri are seasonal rivers.

▼ *An arch constructed on the banks of the Mississippi River, USA*

## The Mississippi River

The Mississippi River is one of the world's longest river systems and the second longest in North America. The river flows through an area of 5,887 kilometres from its source at Lake Itasca in northern Minnesota to the Gulf of Mexico. The name is derived from a native American word that means 'father of waters'. This river system has many creeks, bayous, and other natural drainage networks. The Missouri River is such a tributary. It is about 160 kilometres longer than the Mississippi River. The Mississippi-Missouri combination is the fourth longest river in terms of length. Agriculture is dominant along this river and agricultural industries have developed here.

260 species of fish and 145 species of amphibians and reptiles inhabit the Mississippi River basin. 60 per cent of North American birds use this river basin as their migratory flyway.

## The Amazon River

The Amazon River is located in the continent of South America. It drains practically 40 per cent of South America, thus it is the greatest river of the continent and the largest drainage system in the world. This is because of the volume of its flow and the area of its basin. The total length of the river, as measured from the headwaters of the Ucayali-Apurímac river system in southern Peru, is at least 6,400 kilometres, slightly shorter than the Nile River. It is as long as the distance between New York City and Rome. The mouth of the Amazon River is in the Atlantic Ocean, on the northeastern coast of Brazil.

▲ *There are around 400–500 indigenous Amerindian tribes that live in the Amazon Rainforest. It is believed that about 50 of these tribes have never had contact with the outside world*

## The Congo River

The Congo River lies astride the equator in West Central Africa. This is the second-longest river in Africa. Formerly, it was known as the Zaire River. It drains almost the whole of the Republic of Congo, Democratic Republic of Congo, the Central African Republic; and some parts of Zambia, Angola, Cameroon, and Tanzania. Its source lies in the highlands of North Zambia. It flows into the Atlantic Ocean, at Banane. The Congo River is the main mode of transportation in Central Africa. It is home to a variety of fauna, animals like the Congo peafowl, dryas, crocodiles, elephants, monkeys, and 700 species of marine life.

*The Congo River is the deepest river on Earth. It reaches depths of over 750 feet*

### In Real Life

The Amazon Rainforest is the largest rainforest in the world. It is of great ecological importance as its biomass is capable of absorbing enormous amounts of carbon dioxide. This region is home to thousands of plants and millions of animal species. One-fifth of all of the world's species of birds can be found here. However, deforestation has taken a toll on this lush rainforest. A estimate says that over one-fifth of the total area of the rainforest has been cut down.

## The Amur River

The Amur River is the third-longest river of China. It rises in Russia, flows along the path to Mongolia and reaches China. In China it is called the Heilong Jiang River or 'black dragon'. China and Russia both benefit economically from this river as fishing is the main occupation practised on its waters.

*An aerial view of the Amur River and the Khabarovsk city bridge; the Trans-Siberian railway is built near this river*

## The Paraná River

The Paraná River is located in south-central part of South America. It runs through Brazil, Paraguay, and Argentina. Paraná River, together with its tributaries, forms the larger of the two river systems that drain into the Río de la Plata. It is 4,880 kilometres long and extends from the confluence of the Grande and Paranaíba Rivers in southern Brazil. The Paraguay-Paraná river system covers an area of more than 2.5 million square kilometres. It is the second largest river system in South America, after the Amazon River. The Itaipu Dam on this river was once the largest hydroelectric power station in the world, before the Three Gorges Dam in China came online and replaced its position.

*The Itaipu Dam on the Paraná River*

# Famous Rivers

**History shows us how rivers have been integral to civilisation.** They also play a vital role in the geopolitics, economies and cultures of their bordering regions, and so some rivers are famous across the world today. Let us take a look at a few such rivers.

*The Brahmaputra River originates from the Chemayungdung Glacier in the Himalayas*

## The Brahmaputra River

The Brahmaputra River has different names as it flows through different countries. The river flows in the continent of Asia. It is 2,900 kilometres long.

The name 'Brahmaputra' is used in India. It translates to 'son of Brahma' in Sanskrit; Brahma is a Hindu god. The Brahmaputra rises in the Himalayas, and flows through southwest Tibet, where it is called 'Yarlung Zangbo', and enters India in its northeast border, through the Yarlung Tsangpo Canyon. In India, the Brahmaputra flows from Arunachal Pradesh. It gets the name Brahmaputra from Assam where it flows through the Assam Valley. Here it joins the River Ganga in Bangladesh as Jamuna and drains in the Bay of Bengal. The river forms a vast **delta** here.

The total area drained by this river is approximately 5,80,000 kilometres. The river is important for both irrigation and transportation. It is the lifeline of Assam. However, flooding of this region is also very common. During spring, when the snowcaps melt in the Himalayas, floods are inevitable. They cause destruction of crops and property, and lead to many deaths.

## The Ganga River

The River Ganga (also known as Ganges) runs along the plains of northern India. This river is also a good example of a perennial river. It rises in the Himalayas and drains into the Bay of Bengal. Its length is about 2,510 kilometres, relatively shorter than the other great rivers of the world. But it is of massive importance. It flows through the most fertile and densely populated regions of the world. Millions of people use its water for bathing, drinking, and industrial production.

It is the holy river for the Hindus, and plays an important role in many cultural and religious rites. The River Ganga has a unique ecosystem with 140 species of freshwater fish, 90 amphibian species, and 315 bird species. These are mainly found in the mangroves of the Sundarbans delta in the Bengal Basin.

*The River Ganga in the plains of Bengal*

## The Volga River

The Volga River is located in Europe. It is the longest river of the continent. The river is 3,692 kilometres long and drains almost two-fifths of the European part of Russia. It rises in the Valdai Hills which are in the northwest of Moscow. It discharges into the Caspian Sea. River Volga ranks among the world's greatest rivers due to its immense economic, cultural, and historic importance.

The river valley provides a large amount of wheat. It is also rich in other minerals. There are around 127 species in the river. The Volga **estuary** is the largest in Europe. The river remains frozen for three months in a year during winter.

▲ *River Volga has more than 200 tributaries. The prominent ones are the Rivers Kama, Oka, Vetluga, and Sura*

▲ *The Danube River is a graveyard for sunken German warships from WWII. Sensing defeat, rather than letting the Allies capture their vessels, the Germans scuttled many of them in the river*

## The Danube River

The River Danube is the second-longest river in Europe after Volga. It rises in the Black Forest mountains of western Germany and flows for some 2,850 kilometres to its mouth on the Black Sea. It passes through Germany, Ukraine, Hungary, Moldova, and six other European countries. It is also of great economic value to these 10 countries as it is used for fishing, transport, and hydroelectricity. This river played a vital role in the settlement and political evolution of central and southeastern Europe. Its banks, that are lined with castles and fortresses, formed the boundary between great empires, and its waters served as a vital commercial highway between nations.

## The Zambezi River

The Zambezi River drains the southern portion of Central Africa. It is the fourth-longest river in this continent, flowing for 2,540 kilometres from the Central African Plateau. It empties into the Indian Ocean. On its route, it flows through six African nations including Zambia, Zimbabwe, and Mozambique. Indeed, several disputes have broken out among these countries over the claim to its waters.

▲ *The Victoria Falls on Zambezi River has an output of 550 million litres of water every minute—as much as 200 Olympic-sized swimming pools!*

### Isn't It Amazing!

More than seventy countries celebrate World Rivers Day on the fourth Sunday of September. This global event raises awareness of the importance of rivers and how we can protect them for our better future.

# Cascading Waters

**A waterfall is a place where water flows vertically from a river or another waterbody.** It is a steep fall over a rocky ledge into a plunge pool below. Cascades is another name for waterfalls. When water flows over underlying rocks, it naturally erodes softer rocks like limestone faster than harder rocks like granite, leaving the hard rocks behind. The granite that remains when the soft rock is worn away creates cliffs and ledges.

▲ *The formation of land causes a waterfall. If there is a cliff or ledge naturally, rushing river waters will simply fall over the edge*

## Niagara Falls

Waterfalls are beautiful physical occurrences. There are some that are grand and make our planet even more beautiful. One such waterfall is the Niagara Falls. It is on the Niagara River in North America and is one of the spectacular physical features of the continent of North America. The falls lie on the border between Ontario, Canada, and New York State, USA.

There are two main parts of the falls and they are separated by the Goat Island. It comprises three waterfalls, from largest to smallest, they are: the Horseshoe Falls (also known as the Canadian Falls), American Falls, and Bridal Veil Falls. The height of the Horseshoe Falls is 56 metres and the length of its curving **crest line** is about 670 metres. The American Falls, adjoining the right bank, are 58 metres high and 320 metres across. A huge amount of water flows over Niagara Falls, as much as 5,525 cubic metre per second. This water is used to generate hydroelectric power.

▲ *The length of the Canadian, or Horseshoe brink is 2,600 feet. The horseshoe shape makes the waterfall look smaller, but it is just the opposite*

### Incredible Individuals

Annie Edson Taylor was the first person to go over the Niagara Falls in a barrel on 24 October 1901. She was a school teacher and a brave lady to do this. She died in 1924 and is buried at Oakwood Cemetery in Niagara Falls in an area called Stunter's Rest.

## Victoria Falls

Victoria Falls is another magnificent waterfall. It is also one of the world's mightiest waterfalls located in east-central Africa, on the border between Zambia and Zimbabwe. It is located midway along the course of the Zambezi River. Victoria Falls is about twice as wide and deep as the Niagara Falls. The mist from the falling water is especially dense during the rainy season. It is considered to be the biggest curtain of falling water in the world. The waterfall spans the entire breadth of the Zambezi River and is twice as wide and deep as the Niagara Falls. Approximately, 550 million litres of water drops 93 metres every minute over the cliff at Victoria Falls, and continues flowing downstream as the lower Zambezi River.

▲ *The width of Victoria Falls in the wet season is a bit over 1,609 metres wide*

▲ *Lakes regulate the flow of river water. During the monsoon season they prevent flooding*

# Small Waterbodies

**Apart from the vast oceans, large seas and big rivers, there are some smaller waterbodies on Earth which might be salt water or freshwater.** Some of these are moving and some are contained. They can be distinguished by their shapes and sizes and by the kind of vegetation that thrives within them. The different smaller waterbodies are lakes, ponds, gulfs, bays, and straits.

## Lakes

A lake is a body of water that is full of freshwater. It is surrounded on all of its sides by land. The great lakes in the northern parts of the USA are much larger than the average lake. Some lakes however are salt waterbodies, such as Utah's Great Salt Lake.

Lakes are found everywhere in the world and in all kinds of environments. There are different sizes of lakes and some are so big that they are referred to as seas, for example the Caspian Sea.

## Bay

A bay is a body of water which is partially surrounded by land. It is usually smaller and less enclosed than a gulf. The mouth of the bay, where it meets the ocean, is typically wider than that of a gulf. The Bay of Bengal and the Hudson Bay are examples of bays. Bays are called **lagoons** sometimes. Lagos, the capital of Nigeria, is a bay-side city. It sits on Lagos Lagoon, on the Bight of Benin.

## Strait

A strait is a narrow body of water that acts as a passage between two navigable landmasses. It is formed by natural process. A strait can connect two bigger waterbodies also if it is formed by a fracture in an **isthmus**. These straits are usually formed because of tectonic activity, a matching example being the Strait of Gibraltar. This is the only link between the Mediterranean Sea and the Atlantic Ocean. When fractures in an isthmus are created by human activity, they are usually called canals.

▲ *Ponds support two-thirds of all freshwater species*

## Ponds

A pond can be formed by natural or artificial methods, as compared to seas and lakes. It is a smaller body of water. They are by all means smaller than lakes, though there is no standard or fixed measurement of how big a pond should be. Therefore, many times a big pond can be mistaken for a lake. Ponds are fresh waterbodies and arise naturally in floodplains.

## Gulf

A gulf is a portion of the sea that is surrounded by land on all sides except for one where there is a narrow opening. They are generally larger than bays and are more indented. Gulfs are formed by movements in Earth's crust.

Gulfs can also have wide openings and sometimes cannot be differentiated from larger bodies of water.

▼ *The Suez Canal has made transportation between Europe and Asia easier as it is no longer necessary to go around the entire continent of Africa*

# Natural Lakes

**A lake is a waterbody that is surrounded by land.** There are hundreds and thousands of lakes on Earth. There are two distinct types of lakes—natural and artificial. Natural lakes were formed by glaciers that once covered Earth some 18,000 years ago, during the most recent ice age. Lakes were also formed due to the movements of tectonic plates and as a result of volcanic eruptions. Some lakes are also formed by rivers and landslides. Some of the famous natural lakes are Lake Superior, Lake Victoria, and Lake Baikal.

*The Michigan State Tree and White Pine, along with some 60 species of orchids are native to the Lake Superior area. This lake was formed 1.2 million years ago*

## Lake Superior

One of the greatest natural lakes in the world is Lake Superior in the USA. There are five great lakes in North America, of which Lake Superior is the largest, coldest, and deepest. It is also one of the world's largest bodies of freshwater. It got its name from the French words '*lac supérieur*', which mean 'upper lake'.

Lake Superior is situated on the northern edge of Wisconsin and is bounded by Michigan, Ontario, and Minnesota. The lake is about 257 kilometres wide and 563 kilometres long. The deepest point in Lake Superior is 400 metres below the surface. It is mostly covered with ice in the winters but does not freeze completely. It is the cleanest and clearest of the Great Lakes. Visibility can be about 27 feet. There are many streams and rivers that empty into this lake.

### In Real Life

Over 200 rivers feed Lake Superior. The Nipigon River is one of the largest among them. It has had high waters in the months of October and November. In the months of March and April, it has had low waters.

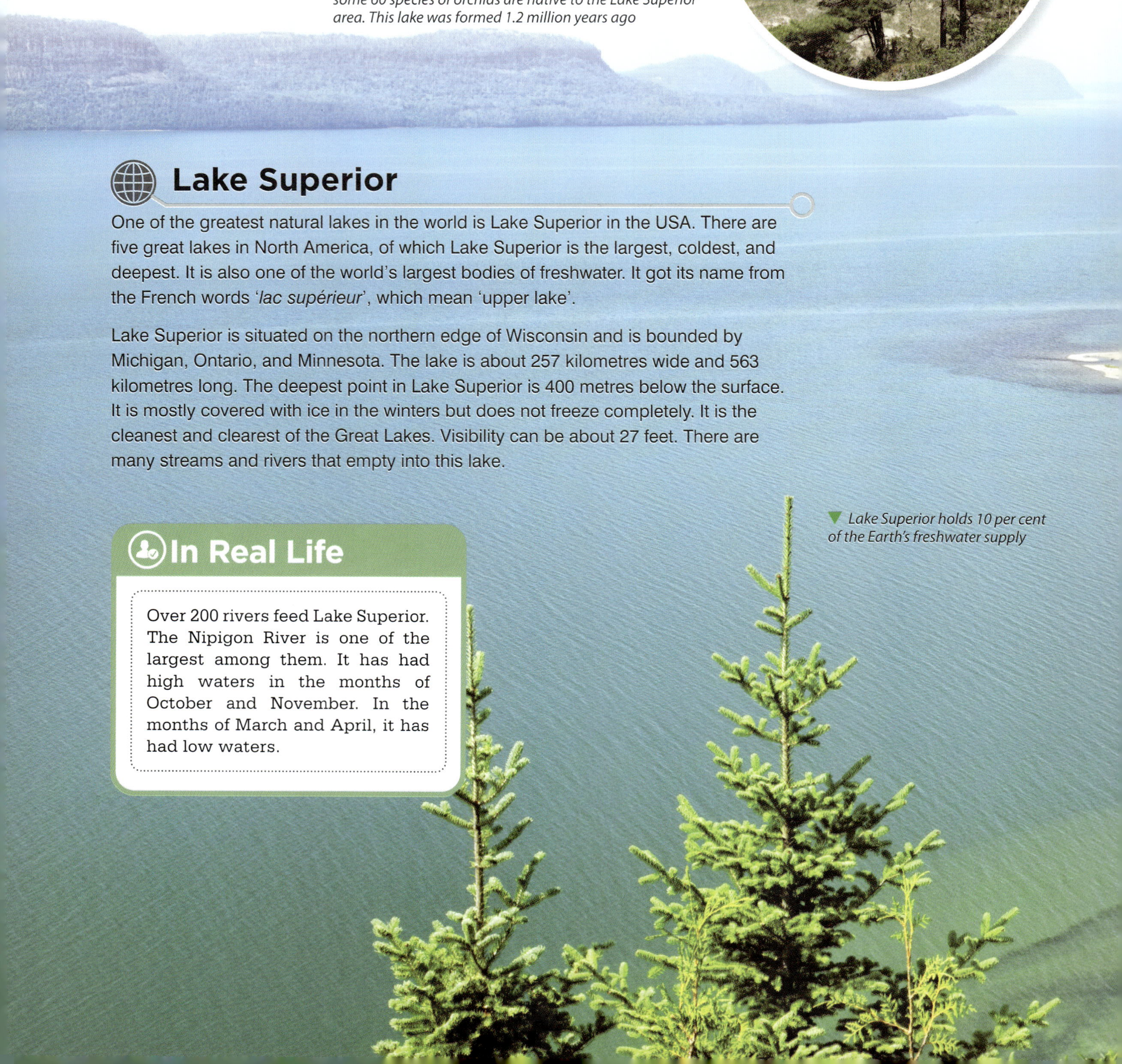

*Lake Superior holds 10 per cent of the Earth's freshwater supply*

▲ *Lake Victoria covers an area of 68,800 square kilometres, making it one of the largest lakes by area, and one of the largest tropical lakes in the world*

## Lake Victoria

Lake Victoria is another famous natural lake. It is the largest in the continent of Africa and is the reservoir of the River Nile. It lies mainly in Tanzania and Uganda. This lake was formed during the upheavals that created the Great Rift Valley 12 million years ago. It is approximately 410 kilometres long and 250 kilometres wide. It is not very deep and occupies a shallow depression (75 metres deep) on the Equatorial Plateau, whose altitude is 3,725 feet. The lake has an irregular shoreline and many small islands. Numerous streams, including the Kagera River, lead into Lake Victoria. This lake is said to be relatively young as its current basin formed only 400,000 years ago. Lake Victoria supports the lives of millions of people living around its shores, in one of the most densely populated regions on Earth.

## Lake Baikal

Lake Baikal is one of the deepest lakes in the world, and is located in Russia. It is the largest in terms of volume. Its surface area is 31,500 square kilometres and it has a length of 636 kilometres and depth of about 1,637 metres.

Lake Baikal is actually located in Siberia within the Republic of Buryatia and the Irkutsk province of Russia. It is the oldest existing freshwater lake on Earth, formed around 20–25 million years old. There are more than 330 rivers and streams that flow into Lake Baikal. It lies in a deep structural hollow surrounded by mountains, some of which are 2,000 metres above the lake's surface. It produces hot mineral springs in the area where there are breaks in the Earth's crust. Occasionally, earthquakes also occur in this region. An earthquake in 1862, in the northern Selenga delta, created a new bay in Baikal known as the Proval Bay.

▼ *There are between 1,500 and 1 800 animal species and hundreds of plant species found in Lake Baikal*

# Artificial Lakes

**Artificial lakes are created by humans.** They are made by digging basins or by damming rivers and springs. These artificial lakes can become reservoirs for storing water for irrigation, hygiene, and industrial use. Artificial lakes are also used for recreational activities such as boating, swimming, and fishing. Some famous artificial lakes are Lake Volta, Lake Williston, and Lake Naseer.

## Lake Volta

Lake Volta is an artificial lake in Ghana. It was formed by the Akosombo Dam whose construction began in 1961 and ended in 1965 on the Volta River. During its construction, a lake was created flowing upstream from the Akosombo Dam to Yapei. Lake Volta is one of the largest artificial lakes in the world. It is about 400 kilometres long and covers an area of 8,502 kilometres. The lake has been used to navigate from the northern Savanna to the coast of Ghana. It is also an important fishing and irrigation source for the fishermen and farmers in the dry Accra Plains lying immediately below the dam.

▼ A view of Lake Volta

## Lake Oahe

The Lake Oahe is created by the Missouri River, in USA. It stretches for 231miles from Oahe Dam near Pierre. It is also the largest of the four Missouri River reservoirs. Its maximum depth is 205 feet. It is good for boating and fishing. The most commonly found species here are smallmouth bass, white bass, northern pike and perch. This is the largest man-made lake in the continent of North America.

▼ A view of Lake Oahe

## Lake Bhojtal

Lake Bhojtal is situated in the west central part of Bhopal, Madhya Pradesh, India. It is surrounded by Van Vihar National Park in the south, human settlements in the east and north, and agriculture fields in the west. The lake has an area of 31 square kilometres. Fishing is an important occupation of inhabitants around the lake and is mainly done on its south-eastern shores. It also serves as the source of water for irrigating a large area.

▼ A view of the sunset in Lake Bhojtal

## In Real Life

There are two possible burial sites located near Lake Oahe's shoreline. These are of the Sitting Bull, a Sioux leader. The shoreline is actually known for containing several cultural artefacts important to different Native American tribes. US law prohibits collecting or damaging them.

▼ *A view of Lake Nasser*

▼ *A road built over Williston Lake*

▼ *Kariba Dam wall*

## Lake Nasser

Lake Nasser, also called Lake Nubia, is a reservoir on the Nile River, in Upper Egypt and North Sudan. This artificial lake was created by the construction of the High Dam at Aswan. The dam was built in 1960s. Lake Nasser is 479 kilometres long and 16 kilometres wide at its widest point. It has a gross capacity of 168,900,000,000 cubic metres. Water that is discharged downstream can irrigate 800,000 acres of land. This lake has a major role to play in Egypt's fishing industry.

## Isn't It Amazing!

During its creation, Lake Nasser threatened to submerge the archaeological sites at Abu Simbel and Philae in Egypt. These sites could have been lost under water had the Egyptian government not intervened by making an appeal to UNESCO, thus saving the loss of these sites.

## Lake Williston

The W.A.C. Bennett Dam led to the formation of Lake Williston, which is one of the largest artificial lakes in the world. It is located in Columbia, Canada. Williston Lake covers an area of 250 kilometres in the Rocky Mountain Trench. It is a man-made lake created when the large hydro-electric project, the W.A.C. Bennett Dam was built in 1968. Williston Lake, is the dam reservoir on three different rivers, the Peace, Parsnip, and Findlay.

## Lake Kariba

Lake Kariba is a lake in central Africa that lies between Zambia and Zimbabwe. It was created by damming the Zambezi River in the Kariba Gorge, 400 kilometres below Victoria Falls, where the river narrows between hills of hard rock. The Kariba Dam's hydroelectric facilities served Zambian cities, the Harare and Bulawayo districts, and the southern part of Zimbabwe after 1960.

# Global Warming

**Global warming is defined as the increase in the average temperature of Earth's air and oceans due to the rising levels of greenhouse gases.** Carbon dioxide is an example of a greenhouse emission. Global warming is leading to drastic and alarming changes in the climate.

*There was a time when thick ice sheets covered the land. This period was called the ice age. The first ice age took place 570 million years ago*

## Changes in Climate

The climate of Earth has gone through many changes such as the melting of glaciers during the ice ages, a period when glaciers covered most of Earth. In recent time, the temperatures have increased and that has caused the sea levels to rise. Global climate has also gone through extremely warm periods. However, all these changes happened gradually, at a very slow pace over thousands of years. The changes happening presently are taking place faster than some living beings can adapt to them. Scientists believe that most of the temperature increase since the mid-20th century is likely due to human activities. The temperature since 1880 has been rising every year by about 0.8° C.

## Greenhouse Effect

Greenhouse gases let the Sun's light shine onto Earth's surface, but they trap the heat that reflects back up into the atmosphere. In this way, they act like the insulating glass walls of a greenhouse. The greenhouse effect keeps Earth's climate comfortable, otherwise the temperature would have been cooler than required and many life forms would freeze, finding it difficult to survive. Greenhouse gas emissions have a wide range of environmental and health consequences. They lead to respiratory diseases caused by smog and air pollution, as well as contributing to climate change by trapping heat.

*Toxic factory emissions contribute negatively to the greenhouse effect*

### In Real Life

Some other consequences of climate change exacerbated by greenhouse emissions include extreme weather, food supply shortages, and increased wildfires.

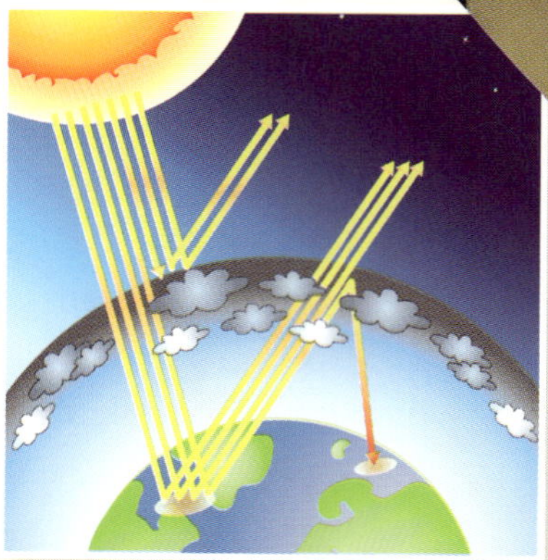

*The diagram shows the greenhouse effect*

▼ *Deforestation is one of the leading causes of global warming*

## Causes of Global Warming

Human beings are responsible for and contribute to global warming by aggravating the greenhouse effect. The effect occurs when certain gases fill up Earth's atmosphere. These include carbon dioxide, methane, nitrogen oxide, and fluorinated gases. Large amounts of these gases are emitted from factories burning fossil fuels such as oil, coal, and natural gas. Even fuels used in transport vehicles add to the problem. Forested areas reduce the amount of carbon dioxide in the atmosphere, but deforestation is cancelling out their effects. In this way, human activities increase the emission of greenhouse gases in the atmosphere, causing global warming. Household appliances such as refrigerators and air conditioners use a lot of energy and emit **refrigerants** that deplete the ozone layer and further contribute to global warming.

## Effects of Global Warming

Effects of global warming are clearly visible today. Human beings, plants and animals are severely affected by changes in their environment. The global ecology is changing too quickly for anyone to adapt. It is triggering natural disasters like floods, tsunamis and earthquakes.

Glaciers are melting and shrinking throughout the world. If the temperature increases, they will continue to melt, which is an alarming sign for wildlife in the polar regions. As the glaciers melt, the ocean levels will rise. This rise in the sea level consequently will lead to frequent floods. Another effect of global warming is the warming of the polar regions due to melting of glaciers. This is making the habitats of some animals warmer. Therefore, these animals are migrating to cooler places. This is also putting some species in danger of extinction.

70 per cent of the Earth is water, so when the oceans heat up, more water evaporates into the clouds which results in heavy and untimely downpours. Storms like hurricanes and typhoons occur much more frequently. Due to untimely rains, crops get destroyed and affect life. Therefore, it is vital to tackle this problem quickly. Otherwise our planet will become a tough place to live in. It is of utmost importance to plant enough trees to counter the greenhouse effect. To reduce emission of greenhouse gases, people should drive less and walk or cycle more. However, changes by individuals are not enough. There needs to be a serious overhaul in our methods of production and consumption.

▲ *Owing to global warming ice breaks off in the polar regions causing the sea levels to rise*

# Word Check

**Aquaculture:** The rearing and cultivation of aquatic animals and plants for food

**Archaea:** They are microorganisms which are similar to bacteria but are radically different in molecular organisation.

**Bacteria:** They are a member of a large group of unicellular microorganisms which have cell walls.

**Brink:** The extreme edge of land before a steep slope or a body or water

**Canyon:** It is a deep gorge that a river flows through.

**Comet:** It is a celestial object consisting of a nucleus of ice and dust that travels near the Sun and develops a tail of gas and dust particles pointing away from the Sun.

**Crest line:** An elongated crest or a linear series of crests

**Delta:** It is a triangular tract of sediment deposited at the mouth of a river, typically where it diverges into several outlets.

**Density:** It is the solidity of a substance.

**Estuary:** It is the mouth of the river where the tide and stream meet.

**Inferno:** It is a large fire that is dangerously out of control.

**Isthmus:** It is a narrow strip of land which has the sea on either side.

**Lagoon:** It is a strip of salt water that is separated from a sea by coral reefs or sandbanks.

**Microscopic:** It describes an organism or substance that is too small to see with the naked eye. It can only be viewed through a microscope.

**Overfishing:** It is when fishermen fish too quickly and too much from one water source, at a rate at which the fish cannot be naturally replaced.

**Refrigerants:** They are working fluids used in the refrigeration cycle of appliances, where they transition from liquid to gas and back.

**Salinity:** It is the quantity of salt that is dissolved in the water.

**Sodium chloride:** It is the chemical name of common salt.

**Tidal bore:** It is a giant wave which moves forward from the sea onto the rivers along with an unusual tide.

**Tributary:** It is the smaller branch of a river flowing into a sea.

**Twilight:** The time after the sun has set and before it gets completely dark